THE 12 WORST
HEALTH DISASTERS
OF ALL TIME

by Susan E. Hamen

www.12StoryLibrary.com

12-Story Library is an imprint of Bookstaves.

Photographs ©: National Museum of Health and Medicine/Armed Forces Institute of Pathology/CC2.5, cover, 1; Art Directors & TRIP/Alamy Stock Photo, 4; Roger Zenner/CC3.0, 5; National Museum of Health and Medicine/Armed Forces Institute of Pathology/CC2.5, 6; Library of Congress, 7; Adam Jan Figel/Shutterstock.com, 8; CREATISTA/Shutterstock.com, 9; Petar Milošević/CC4.0, 10; PD, 11; Tom Kirn, Ron Taylor, Louisa Howard - Dartmouth Electron Microscope Facility/PD, 12; World Health Organization/US National Library of Medicine, 13; T. S. Satyan/World Health Organization/US National Library of Medicine, 14; Wellcome Images/CC4.0, 15; Wellcome Images/CC4.0, 16; Georg Paul Busch/PD, 17; Scanpix/PD, 18; Daily Herald Archive/SSPL/Getty Images, 19; Peteri/Shutterstock.com, 20; frank60/Shutterstock.com, 20; punghi/Shutterstock.com, 21; Bettmann/Getty Images, 22; William Birch/PD, 23; US National Library of Medicine, 24; Internet Archive Book Images/CC, 25; Wellcome Images/CC4.0, 26; Wellcome Images/CC4.0, 27; Fotos593/Shutterstock.com, 28; Alexander Raths/Shutterstock.com, 29

ISBN
978-1-63235-537-9 (hardcover)
978-1-63235-602-4 (paperback)
978-1-63235-656-7 (ebook)

Library of Congress Control Number: 2018946729

Printed in the United States of America
Mankato, MN
June 2018

About the Cover

Camp Funston's emergency military hospital near Junction City, Kansas. Some experts believe the flu pandemic began here in 1918.

Access free, up-to-date content on this topic plus a full digital version of this book. Scan the QR code on page 31 or use your school's login at 12StoryLibrary.com.

Table of Contents

The Black Death Arrives in Europe

There were so many victims they had to be buried in mass graves.

In October 1347, Italian trade ships arrived in Sicily. They were returning from the Middle East. Officials soon made a shocking discovery. Most men on the ships were dead. Surviving sailors were very sick. They showed fever, chills, and vomiting.

Their skin was covered in black boils.

A serious illness was to blame. Officials ordered the ships to leave. They did not want the disease to spread. But it was too late. The Black Death had arrived in Europe. The name came from the black boils appearing on the skin. Others called the illness the Great Plague. Whatever name people used, the bubonic plague was deadly.

The disease was caused by bacteria in rats and fleas. Sailors who were bitten became ill. The disease then spread between people. The Black Death soon advanced to France and North Africa. People in London and Northern Europe began dying.

Spread of the Bubonic Plague in Europe (1347–1351)

- 1347
- mid-1348
- early 1349
- late 1349
- 1350
- 1351
- after 1351
- minor outbreak
- center of uprisings
- city for orientation

Copenhagen
Lübeck
London
Bruges
Brunswick
Magdeburg
Warsaw
Rouen
Frankfurt
Prague
Paris
Vienna
Bucharest
Milan
Ravenna
Marseilles
Florence
Thessaloniki
Toledo
Barcelona
Rome
Athens

People infected by bubonic plague often died within a day of becoming sick. No medicine could cure them. Doctors feared treating the sick. They did not want to be infected. Families were often forced to leave sick loved ones to die.

The Black Death would kill 25 million Europeans by 1351. In just four years, the plague reduced the population of the continent by more than half.

200
Years before Europe's population reached pre-plague numbers.

- Bubonic plague arrived in Sicily on trade ships in 1347.
- The Black Death quickly spread across Europe.
- An estimated 25 million people died during the pandemic.

Flu Pandemic Infects One-Third of the World

It was 1918. World War I was coming to a close. But another type of war was about to begin. The enemy would kill more people than the Great War itself. It was a war against infectious disease.

In the fall of the year, people started feeling sick. The symptoms weren't bad at first. For some people, it felt like coming down with a cold.

But this disease was deadly. It spread very quickly. It raged across Europe, Asia, Africa, North America, and South America.

People ages 20–40 were most affected. This wasn't normal. The flu is usually worst in elderly people and children. Some people who became sick died within hours. There was no cure for the disease.

Some experts say the flu began at an army base in Kansas. Troops trained there carried the virus to Europe. Others say it began in East Asia or Europe. After 18 months and two big waves, the flu ended. Infected people either died or became immune.

About 500 million people were infected. That was one-third of the world's population at the time. Between 20 and 40 million people died.

20
Percent of people who died after being infected.

- The flu spread very quickly.
- The disease was worst for people 20 to 40 years of age.
- Half a billion people infected.

A MISLEADING NICKNAME

The flu pandemic of 1918 is often called the Spanish flu. For this reason, many people still believe the pandemic began in Spain. It did not. But because Spain was neutral in World War I, it didn't have news blackouts. People read in the news that Spain was being hit hard by the flu. So they thought the disease started there and spread to other countries.

Red Cross workers practice at an emergency ambulance station during the 1918 pandemic.

HIV/AIDS Pandemic Infects 70 Million People

In 1981, doctors made an alarming discovery. People were dying of illnesses that were not usually fatal. Patients could not fight off sickness and get better.

Researchers found the virus responsible. They named it human immunodeficiency virus (HIV). People with HIV later developed a more serious condition. It was called acquired immunodeficiency syndrome (AIDS).

Researchers found that HIV is spread through certain body fluids. The virus attacks a person's immune system. This makes it hard for a person to fight illness. When infections develop in the weakened body, a person has AIDS.

A boy is tested for HIV with a blood test.

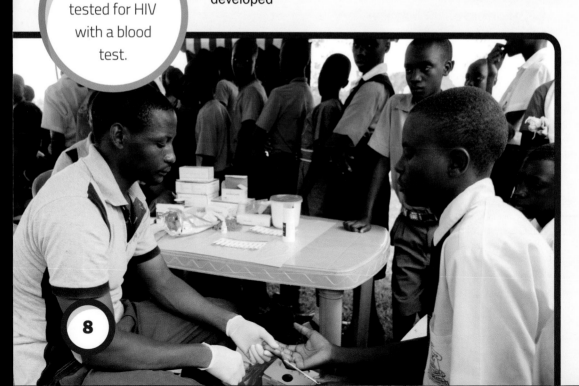

HIV/AIDS started in the African country of Cameroon. Scientists believe the first human infection occurred in the 1930s. People got HIV from eating infected chimpanzee meat.

In 2016, more than 36 million people worldwide were living with HIV. Since the pandemic began, 70 million people have been infected. An estimated 35 million have died. Education about the disease and new medications have slowed its spread.

OUTBREAKS, EPIDEMICS, AND PANDEMICS

An outbreak occurs when a disease infects large numbers of people. Some outbreaks last for days. Others last for years. An epidemic is when a disease spreads quickly to many people. A pandemic occurs when a disease goes worldwide.

2 million

Approximate number of children living with HIV in 2016.

- HIV/AIDS is a virus that weakens a person's immune system.
- The first humans infected got HIV from eating chimpanzee meat.
- About 35 million people have died from HIV/AIDS.

Justinian Plague Is Blow to Byzantine Empire

In the sixth century, the Byzantine Empire included parts of Europe, Africa, and Asia. The emperor, Justinian I, was ambitious. He wanted to conquer more land. But in 541 CE, bubonic plague struck. Justinian now had to fight for the survival of his empire.

Experts believe plague spread through the food supply. Rats with the disease were carried over trade routes.

People infected quickly became very sick. They experienced fever, vomiting, and chills. Most died quickly. No medicine could help. The death rate was very high in the capital city of Constantinople. In the spring of 542, as many as 5,000 people died each day. Nearly half the city's residents perished.

Emperor Justinian was more fortunate. He survived the plague. But any dreams of Byzantine expansion were over. His empire was devastated by what became known as the Justinian Plague. The disease also spread to other areas of the world. Within 50 years, as many as 100 million people in Europe and Asia had died from the sickness.

Emperor Justinian.

THINK ABOUT IT

Do you think a pandemic like the Justinian plague could spread around the world today? How might modern science prevent that from happening? Research the subject online.

50

Estimated percent of Europe's population that died in the plague.

- Justinian I wanted to expand the Byzantine Empire, but bubonic plague struck.
- People in Constantinople and throughout the empire died in large numbers.
- The Justinian plague ended the emperor's hopes for expansion.

As many as 5,000 people died each day in Constantinople.

Cholera Sickens People Across Asia

In August 1817, a surgeon near Calcutta, India, grew alarmed. Many patients coming to him were very sick. They had symptoms of vomiting and diarrhea. Some quickly became dehydrated and died.

It was cholera. The surgeon discovered it was being spread by contaminated rice. Cholera was soon reported throughout India. People in other countries started to get sick, too. Within ten years, cholera was common in Asia.

Cholera is spread when people drink water or eat food contaminated with choleric human feces. The bacteria that cause cholera are often found in areas with poor sanitation systems. This includes developing nations and natural disaster zones. Often there is no fresh water or clean sanitation.

Cholera became widespread in Asia partly because British soldiers in the region carried it to conflict zones. The disease spread to members of opposing forces. They then carried it to new places on the continent.

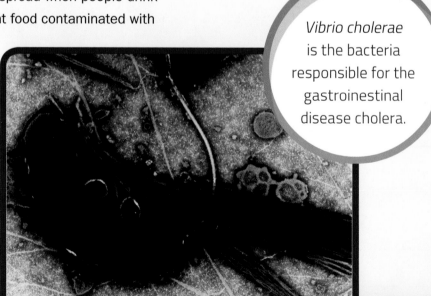

Vibrio cholerae is the bacteria responsible for the gastroinestinal disease cholera.

Nurses attach an intravenous line to rehydrate a patient with cholera.

6.3
**Gallons of fluid (24 L)
a choleric patient can lose
in one day.**

- A surgeon near Calcutta discovered cases of cholera in the area.
- The disease quickly spread around India and into other countries.
- Cholera is common in areas without fresh water or clean sanitation.

CHOLERA IS STILL A CONCERN

Cholera affects people around the world to this day. Since the first outbreak in 1817, it has killed millions. Each year, between 3 and 5 million new cases of cholera are reported. As many as 120,000 people die from the disease each year.

6

World's First Vaccine Leads to End of Smallpox

People don't worry about smallpox today. But for more than 3,000 years, the disease was feared around the world.

Smallpox symptoms include body aches, fever, and a rash. Fluid-filled bumps appear on the skin. Touching bedsheets or clothing with this fluid on it can cause infection. Coughing and sneezing can also transmit the disease.

Smallpox killed millions of people worldwide before 1796. That's when a breakthrough came. English doctor Edward Jenner collected pus from a cowpox rash. He injected it into a healthy person. The pus prevented smallpox. This experiment led to the world's first vaccine.

Use of the vaccine was widespread. Still, people got smallpox into the twentieth century. Nearly 300 million people died of smallpox during the 1900s alone. But progress was made. By 1980, the World Health Organization (WHO) declared that smallpox had been eradicated. It remains the only human disease to be completely wiped out.

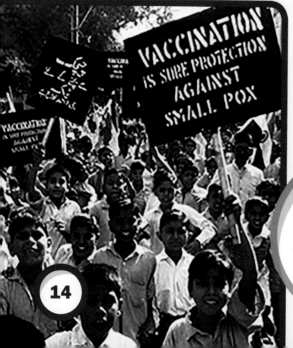

Children carry signs urging vaccination against smallpox.

Edward Jenner M.D.

5 million

Estimated number of lives saved each year by smallpox vaccine.

- Smallpox existed for more than 3,000 years.
- The disease causes body aches, fever, and a rash of fluid-filled bumps on the skin.
- WHO declared smallpox wiped out in 1980.

WHAT DISEASE WILL BE DESTROYED NEXT?

Many diseases hurt human health. Vaccines exist for some of them. But completely wiping out diseases has been very difficult. It can be hard to get medicine to some areas. Still, health officials are trying to end illnesses. Polio, measles, and malaria are some of the diseases that have been targeted for eradication.

15

Antonine Plague Ravages Roman Empire

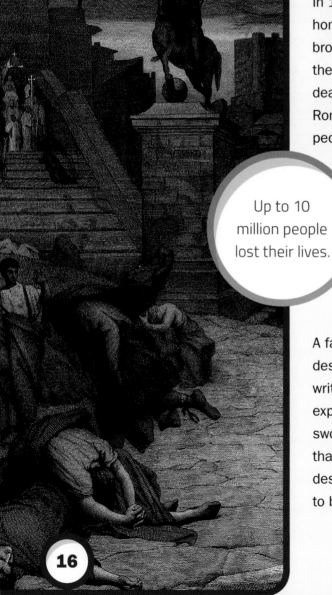

In 165 CE, Roman troops returned home from the Middle East. They brought something unexpected with them. Many were infected with a deadly disease. When they reached Rome, the illness spread. Millions of people would eventually die.

Up to 10 million people lost their lives.

The first wave of the Antonine plague lasted about five years. Four years later, it flared up again. This second outbreak caused up to 2,000 deaths a day in Rome.

A famous physician named Galen described the disease in his writings. Galen wrote that people experienced diarrhea, fever, and a swollen throat. He also reported that patients had skin boils. Galen's descriptions have led many experts to believe it was smallpox.

15

Years the Antonine plague was active in ancient Rome.

- Roman soldiers returning from the Middle East brought home a deadly disease.
- People suffered from diarrhea, fever, a swollen throat, and skin boils.
- The plague hurt the army, limited food production, and stopped building projects.

GALENVS

The Antonine plague had a great impact on the Roman Empire. A once powerful army lost countless men to disease. Many farmers were unable to tend their crops. This meant there was not enough food to feed everyone. Building projects also stopped. There were not enough healthy brickmakers to complete them.

By the time the Antonine plague died out, up to 10 million people had lost their lives. The Roman Empire would never regain its former power. In fact, many experts believe the plague contributed to its fall.

Asian Flu Circles the Globe

Each year, millions of people around the world become ill with flu. But only a small percentage of them die. Most have immunity against the type of flu being spread.

The flu season gets much more dangerous when a new strain of influenza develops. This occurred in 1957. That's when the H2N2 strain caused a pandemic. People had no immunity against the new virus. Millions around the world quickly became sick. Many died.

The pandemic began in China in February 1957. Thousands became ill. The sickness was called the Asian flu. Within a

In 1957, as a result of the Asian flu, this teacher had only one well student able to attend class.

month, 100,000 cases had been reported in Taiwan. And by June, over a million people in India became infected.

The Asian flu circled the globe within five months. Pregnant women, children, and the elderly were most at risk. The H2N2 strain caused a deadly pneumonia. By 1958, an estimated 2 million people had died.

Great Britain was hit hard. Nine million people became ill. About 14,000 died. More than 5 million others needed medical care. Factories, offices, and mines closed. People were too sick to work. The British economy ground to a halt during the pandemic.

D S White   24/9/57
7.. The typist with a new look takes care not to catch Asian Flu , as she wears one of the masks being sold for the purpose in Manchester........

CAN A SHOT STOP FLU INFECTIONS?

Each year, health officials create a vaccine to prevent flu. Many people get this vaccine. But it doesn't always work. The effectiveness of the vaccine varies from year to year. It depends on how well flu strains in the vaccine match the ones making people sick.

12
Years it took for H2N2 flu strain to disappear from the human population.

- New flu strains are more dangerous because people are not immune to them.
- The Asian flu pandemic began in China and quickly spread around the world.
- An estimated 2 million people lost their lives to the disease.

9

Malaria Deaths Date Back 4,000 Years

Malaria has affected humans for more than 4,000 years. Over that time, many large epidemics have occurred. Millions of people have died from the disease.

Malaria is caused by a parasite. Mosquitoes spread it to people. The disease is most common in hot places with a lot of mosquitoes. Sub-Saharan Africa has the most malaria cases by far. Of the 212 million cases in 2015, 90 percent occurred there. South Asia also has many infections.

Malaria patients experience fever, chills, and other flu-like symptoms. Left untreated, the disease can be deadly. Medications can stop malaria. But often people cannot get them. Hundreds of thousands die from malaria each year.

Part of the problem is poverty. It

MALARIA AROUND THE WORLD

- malaria transmission occurs
- limited risk
- no malaria

is often difficult for people living in poverty to buy medicine. People can be bit by infected mosquitoes as they sleep. But it might be impossible to get sleeping nets.

People with malaria are often too sick to work. Kids can't attend school. This hurts families and the society. High health care costs hurt the economy. Tourists are often afraid to travel to places with malaria. This stops outside money from coming in.

There is not yet a vaccine for malaria. Researchers are trying to find one now. Nearly half of the

29

Percent reduction in malaria death rates globally since 2010.

- Malaria is caused by a parasite that mosquitoes spread.
- Sub-Saharan Africa has the most cases of malaria.
- Malaria hurts families and the greater society.

world's population is at risk of the disease. A vaccine could protect them. The goal is to wipe out malaria.

Yellow Fever Attacks Philadelphia

Carriages collected the dying and the dead.

200,000
Annual cases of yellow fever worldwide.

- Yellow fever is caused by a virus spread by infected mosquitoes.
- Up to 5,000 Philadelphians died of yellow fever in 1793.
- A vaccine has helped reduce the number of cases worldwide.

THINK ABOUT IT

During the yellow fever outbreak in Philadelphia, doctors did not know how the disease spread. Could they have prevented deaths if they knew mosquitoes transmitted the disease?

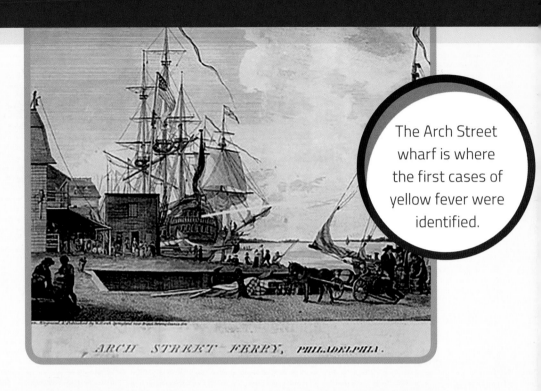

ARCH STREET FERRY, PHILADELPHIA.

The Arch Street wharf is where the first cases of yellow fever were identified.

In 1793, Philadelphia, Pennsylvania, was a busy city. It served as the capital of the new United States while Washington, DC, was being built. Businesses there thrived. However, an outbreak of yellow fever soon brought activity to a halt.

The disease came from the Caribbean. French refugees from the island of Santo Domingo brought the disease. Shortly after, Philadelphia residents began to get sick. Mosquitoes had spread the yellow fever.

Symptoms of yellow fever include muscle aches, vomiting, weakness, fever, and bleeding. The liver and kidneys stop functioning. This causes the skin to look yellow, giving the disease its name.

In October of 1793, as many as 100 people were dying each day. Some fled the city to avoid catching the disease. But many could not. Between August and November, up to 5,000 people died. This was ten percent of the population. Finally, cold weather arrived and killed off the infected mosquitoes.

Today, there is a vaccine for yellow fever. But access to the vaccine is limited in some parts of the world. About 30,000 people still die of yellow fever each year. Ninety percent of these cases are in Africa.

11

Russian Flu Rides the Rails and Sails the Seas

In November 1889, many people in St. Petersburg, Russia, became ill. The sickness seemed a lot like flu. But symptoms of fever, body aches, coughing, and sore throat were more severe than usual. By December, the Russian flu had infected 150,000 people. It caused a record number of deaths in the city.

Soon the virus began to spread. It did so

70

Days it took the Russian flu to spread from Russia to the United States.

- The Russian flu pandemic of 1889 began in St. Petersburg, Russia.
- Railroads and shipping routes helped the quick spread of the virus.
- The pandemic killed about 1 million people worldwide.

Special tents were set up to care for the sick.

The growing railway system in Russia contributed to the spread of the flu.

quickly. The nineteenth century had brought rapid growth to urban areas. People lived closer together. It was easier for the virus to spread.

Another factor in its quick spread was the growing railway system. Large numbers of people were able to travel great distances in short amounts of time. People exposed to the Russian flu carried it to other places on rail lines.

By the fall of 1890, the Russian flu had spread to North and South America, Australia, and Africa on shipping routes. Within one year, the pandemic had circled the globe. An estimated 1 million people worldwide died from the flu.

THINK ABOUT IT

The Russian flu was spread by people who traveled on trains and ships. Today airplanes transport people around the world. How might air travel affect the spread of infectious diseases?

Bubonic Plague Persists for a Century

Several pandemics of bubonic plague have struck humanity. The last began in 1855. It started in China's Yunnan province. People got the disease from infected rats and fleas. The disease then spread along trade routes. By 1894, the plague reached Hong Kong. Infected rats aboard steamships then carried it to India.

The outbreak of plague in India affected millions. British officials who ruled India asked a microbiologist to create a vaccine. In 1897, Waldemar Haffkine was successful. But British officials did not give him the necessary resources. He could not offer the vaccine on a large scale. Haffkine vaccinated many people in India. But the effort was not enough to stop the disease.

A person with bubonic plague in India, 1897.

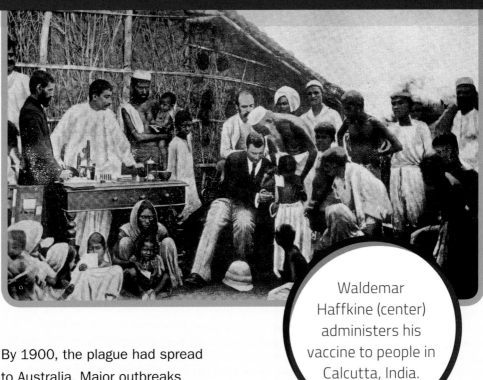

Waldemar Haffkine (center) administers his vaccine to people in Calcutta, India.

By 1900, the plague had spread to Australia. Major outbreaks occurred in shipping ports around that country. Hundreds died. Ships carried the plague to Japan, Egypt, South Africa, Hawaii, Great Britain, France, and many other areas. Sickness and death circled the globe. For the next 50 years, the plague continued to infect people. Doctors gave vaccines in hard-hit areas to stop it. Finally, in 1959, the modern pandemic came to an end. An estimated 15 million people had died.

Localized outbreaks of plague still occur in places like China, India, and Africa. But the pandemic is over.

2,000
Average number of yearly cases of bubonic plague that occur today.

- Infected rats in China's Yunnan province caused a modern pandemic.
- A vaccine was developed in 1897, but infections continued.
- The modern plague killed an estimated 15 million people globally.

Staying Safe If There Is a Health Disaster

- Stock up on essential supplies in case of a quarantine. Collect items such as canned foods, granola bars, peanut butter, dried fruit, and bottled water.

- Have a plan in place. Talk to family members about how you should respond if a health emergency occurs.

- If a known outbreak or epidemic reaches your community, cover your mouth and nose if you go outside. Use a surgical mask to protect yourself.

- Establish healthy habits that reduce the spread of disease. Wash your hands frequently. Cover your mouth and nose when you cough and sneeze.

- Record the name and number of your doctor, clinic, and pharmacy. Have this info in an easy to find location.

- If you take medication, keep a supply on hand. Have enough available to stay healthy if you are unable to leave your home for several days.

- Make a list of your essential health information. Include allergies, medical conditions, blood type, and other details.

- If you are sick, stay home. Don't go to school or work.

Glossary

bacteria
Microscopic organisms that can cause disease.

boil
Painful inflammation of the skin that is usually filled with fluid.

epidemic
The rapid spread of a disease to many people in one area.

feces
The solid waste your body releases.

immunity
The ability to resist an infection because of previous exposure to the disease.

news blackouts
Times when certain types of news are censored by the government.

outbreak
Episode of a disease infecting greater numbers of people than usual in an area.

pandemic
Health disaster in which a disease spreads throughout the world.

parasite
An organism that lives on or in another organism.

pneumonia
An inflammation of the lungs that can cause them to fill with fluid.

pus
A thick yellowish liquid that forms in infected body tissue.

strain
A particular type of disease or infection.

vaccine
A substance preventing the spread of disease.

virus
Tiny molecules that cause big diseases. A disease or illness caused by a virus.

For More Information

Books

Platt, Richard. *Plagues, Pox, and Pestilence.* New York: Kingfisher, 2011.

Rolfes, Nina. *Examining Pandemics.* Minneapolis, MN: Clara House Books, 2015.

Throp, Claire. *The Horror of the Bubonic Plague.* Portsmouth, NH: Heinemann, 2017.

Visit 12StoryLibrary.com

Scan the code or use your school's login at **12StoryLibrary.com** for recent updates about this topic and a full digital version of this book. Enjoy free access to:

- Digital ebook
- Breaking news updates
- Live content feeds
- Videos, interactive maps, and graphics
- Additional web resources

Note to educators: Visit 12StoryLibrary.com/register to sign up for free premium website access. Enjoy live content plus a full digital version of every 12-Story Library book you own for every student at your school.

Index

About the Author

Susan E. Hamen has written more than 30 books for children on various topics, including the Wright brothers, World War II, and ancient Rome. Hamen lives in Minnesota with her husband, daughter, and son.

READ MORE FROM 12-STORY LIBRARY

Every 12-Story Library Book is available in many fomats. For more information, visit 12StoryLibrary.com